Hotel Paris

CATALAN STUDIES IN CULTURE AND LINGUISTICS

Edited by
Antonio Cortijo Ocaña

VOLUME 7

PETER LANG

Berlin · Bruxelles · Chennai · Lausanne · New York · Oxford

HOTEL PARIS

Vicent Andrés Estellés

Edition, Foreword and Translation
by DOMINIC KEOWN

Berlin · Bruxelles · Chennai · Lausanne · New York · Oxford

Library of Congress Cataloging-in-Publication
A CIP record for this book has been applied for at the Library of Congress.

Bibliographic information published by the Deutsche Nationalbibliothek
The Deutsche Nationalbibliothek lists this publication in the Deutsche
Nationalbibliografie; detailed bibliographic data is available on the
Internet at http://dnb.d-nb.de.

This study was carried out within the framework of the Institut Superior d'Investigació Cooperativa IVITRA [ISIC-IVITRA] (Programa per a la Constitució i Acreditació d'Instituts Superiors d'Investigació Cooperativa d'Excel·lència de la Generalitat Valenciana, Ref. ISIC/012/042), based at the Universitat d'Alacant/University of Alicante [UA]. This translation has received economic help from the Institut Ramon Llull [IRL]. This book and the scientific work involved with it as well as the dissemination of its results has special support within the Institució Alfons el Magnànim-Centre Valencià d'Estudis i d'Investigació [IAM], and the following research projects and groups: MICINUN, Ref. PID2021-128381NB-I00; PROMETEO/2023/6 (Programa Prometeo de la Generalitat Valenciana per a grups d'investigació d'excel·lència); IEC-Institut d'Estudis Catalans (Delegació d'Alacant); Grup d'Investigació VIGROB-125 of the UA; Grup d'Investigació en Tecnologia Educativa en Història de la Cultura, Diacronia lingüística i Traducció (Universitat d'Alacant, Ref. GITE-09009-UA]); Center For Catalan Studies (University of California at Santa Barbara / UA); Facultat de Filosofia i Lletres de la UA; Servei de Llengües de la UA; Departament de Filologia Catalana i Lingüística General de la Universitat de les Illes Balears; and the Venue of the University of Alicante at la Nucia (Alacant/Alicante).

ISSN 2627-468X
ISBN 978-3-631-92362-7 (Print)
E-ISBN 978-3-631-92360-3 (E-PDF)
E-ISBN 978-3-631-92361-0 (EPUB)
DOI 10.3726/b22119

© 2024 Peter Lang Group AG, Lausanne
Published by Peter Lang GmbH, Berlin, Germany

info@peterlang.com – www.peterlang.com

All rights reserved.

All parts of this publication are protected by copyright.
Any utilization outside the strict limits of the copyright
law, without the permission of the publisher, is forbidden and liable to prosecution.
This applies in particular to reproductions, translations, microfilming,
and storage and processing in electronic retrieval systems.

Contents

Acknowledgements 7

Introduction 9

L'Hotel París / Hotel Paris 24

Bibliography 71

Acknowledgements

The present edition has been made possible by the generous collaboration and permission of the Estellés family in Burjassot, the Grup Enciclopèdia from Barcelona, John Benjamins of Amsterdam/Philadelphia, Peter Lang of Berlin, Bruxelles, Chennai, Laussane, New York, Oxford and Vicent Martines, director of ISIC-IVITRA, at the University of Alacant [UA]/ Seu Universitària de la Nucia (UA).

Thanks are also due to the much missed Robin Warner, for his revision of the translation, Bryan Cameron, for his comments on the Introduction, and Irene Mira and Jordi Oviedo for their help and cooperation.

Introduction

> For Robin Warner and Vicent Salvador:
> *"verray, parfit, gentil knights."*

Vicent Andrés Estellés was born on September 4, 1924, into a family of bakers in the village of Burjassot, five miles north-west of Valencia. His education and upbringing were, in this way, thoroughly immersed in the agricultural lifestyle at the heart of this famous green belt (*l'horta*). And, as with Seamus Heaney, Dylan Thomas, Ted Hughes and other artists from the periphery, the ethos would condition his output significantly. As an infant, the poet lived through the military dictatorship of Primo de Rivera (1923–1930). This centralist autocracy, with its arcane obsession with the essential unity of Spain and the consequent proscription of non-Castilian languages and cultures, would be brushed aside by the popular mobilisation which brought into existence the reformist II Republic in 1931. Herein, democratic purpose, truly experienced for the first time in the contemporary history of Spain, was exemplified by the recognition of national plurality in the Statutes of Autonomy for Catalonia in 1932 and Euzkadi four years later. Similar devolution proposed for Galicia and Valencia was interrupted, along with other progressive measures, by General Franco's act of rebellion which brought about the outbreak of Civil War in 1936.

Though the poet was to witness the severity of this conflict in his early teens it would be the brutality of its aftermath which would take centre stage in his creative output. Indeed many commentators have referred to his verse as a chronicle of the hardship and deprivation of the post-war period. These years were not only ravaged by starvation, shortages, penury, rationing, the scourge of corruption and the pervasive black market but were also subjected to the tyranny of a military dictatorship whose repression was ruthless. For a region like Valencia, which had fought on the losing side of the conflict, the subjugation was particularly vengeful. With its historical difference and potential alternative affiliation to Catalonia in terms of language, culture and history, the community constituted a threat to a key point of the *Generalísimo*'s crusade: the fanatical belief in the "sacred" homogeneity of Spain.

In this environment of deprivation and fascist hysteria, Estellés won a scholarship in 1942 to study journalism in Madrid where he remained for the three years of the course until compulsory military service took him to Navarre in 1945 before a return home to Valencia. In 1948 he began work as a reporter on the staff of *Las Provincias*, one of the local dailies, of which he would become editor ten years later. This period would mark a defining moment in the personal, creative and political development of the poet. It is in the early 1950s, for example, that his first serious works in the vernacular begin to take shape, albeit clandestinely, given the heartless repression visited upon all non-Castilian languages by Franco's state machinery. Like Seamus Heaney, much of his output functions as a journal of life in the locality during the period: a commitment to his community and a disturbing denunciation of the injustices suffered.

The harshness of Franco's repression meant that, despite the enormity of the poet's production during this and the following decade, only a handful of collections appeared in print. The unpublished material, stored chaotically in the author's study, was to see the light of day subsequently in the forty-two collections which appeared between 1970 and the poet's death in 1993. The total does not include the ten volumes of the Complete Poetry, whose edition was started in 1972, and the immensity of the *magnum opus* of the *Mural del País Valencià* (Mural of the Land of Valencia) whose two voluminous tomes were initiated in 1974, appearing posthumously in 1994. At the time of writing, a revised edition of the Complete Poetry is nearing completion.

It was precisely in the 1950s, however, that Estellés became one of the major figures in the cultural resistance to the dictatorship not only through his covert verse in the vernacular but also his friendship and association with prominent apologists for the Catalan cause in Valencia. In 1955, the poet married Isabel Lorente and their first child, a daughter, was born ten months later although she was to die shortly afterwards. The bereavement was devastating. Its traumatic consequences, however, would have a positive dimension. The pain caused by this tragic loss would increase the poet's awareness of the suffering endured by his community under the dictatorship. Happily, two other children were to follow to enrich a marriage which would become a cornerstone of the personal, creative and social life of the writer.

After the severity of the repression of the first two decades of the dictatorship the situation was to ease marginally in the 1960s. Spain's economy was to improve with the advent of tourism and mass emigration to a Europe in the full swing of post-war recovery. And the need of the regime to present a more human face to the holiday market of the continent allowed for a minimal relaxation in censorship and other repressive strictures. In this ambience—as in the North of Ireland during the same period—there was popular mobilisation in support of social progress and Civil Rights. And a crucial publication in 1962, *Nosaltres, els valencians* (Ourselves, the Valencians) by Joan Fuster, traced the Catalan basis to the history, language and creative personality of the region. And his analysis contained an implicit political, administrative and cultural rapprochement with Catalonia along the progressive and democratic lines of a shared national consciousness. The monograph was to inspire and add cohesion to popular and political support for the radical agenda.

As might be expected, the thesis was to prove anathema to the die-hard defenders of Spanish unity in Valencia who, in line with their Francoist patrons, considered any such cultural and linguistic realignment as a herald of the disintegration of the state and its alleged unitarian destiny. The stand-off between the two factions was to give rise to the notorious *Batalla de València* (Battle of Valencia) a conflict which not only scarred the locality for decades but has, in fact, been rekindled with the victory of the conservative and neo-Francoist Right in the autonomous and municipal elections of 2023.

From its power base in local government the reactionary element attempts to control the mindset of the community, as it had done previously, via a veritable *Kulturkampf*. Through patronage of academically dubious organisations, intimidation, and campaigns against the autochthonous language, it engenders and sustains a rabid anti-Catalanist sentiment with the aim of precluding the potential re-alignment envisioned by Fuster's thesis. A touchstone of such abject prejudice is the official insistence by parties on the Right that the vernacular of Valencia is not Catalan but a completely distinct idiom. This is despite the insistence of linguistic unity endorsed by every Faculty of Philology and Modern Languages the world over.[1]

In this ambience of coercion, the most disgraceful atrocities were to occur. During the early years of the new democratic era, the Francoist bunker attempted to eradicate growing Catalanist sympathies once and for all. And Estellés was to suffer particularly. After winning the *Premi d'Honor de les Lletres Catalanes* in 1978, the most prestigious award bestowed by Catalonia to authors in that language, the poet was summarily removed from the editorship of *Las Provincias* and left in virtual destitution as anonymous threats were levelled against him. The electoral success of the progressive Socialist party (PSOE) in 1983 signified a temporary change in fortunes in institutional terms as Estellés was awarded the the *Premi de les Lletres Valencianes* in 1984. A modest pension was also granted to the destitute writer by the autonomous government though the hostility orchestrated against him by recalcitrant Francoist sentiment was to pursue him until his death in 1993. The same venom was directed against his friend and

---

1 The socio-linguistic situation of Catalan throughout its territories is outlined by Miquel Strubell, "The Catalan Language", in *Companian to Catalan Culture*, ed. by Dominic Keown (London: Boydell and Brewer, 2011), pp. 117–142.

apologist for the Catalan identity of Valencia, Joan Fuster. In 1981, right-wing terrorists planted two bombs in his house. And even in death the historian was allowed no peace as, in 1997, his tomb was desecrated during the celebration of the 75th anniversary of his birth. The statue of Estellés erected in the town hall square in his native Burjassot has similarly been the continuous victim of neo-Francoist vandalism.

Sadly, therefore, in a return to the vindictive politico-cultural ethos of the 1970s, the Battle of Valencia is as alive as ever. Official funding has been removed from those entities which promote the autochthonous language and culture. To this effect, the silence from the autonomous and municipal government in Valencia regarding celebration of the centenary of the poet's birth in 2024 has been deafening. In the face of such official hostility, however, universities, schools and, most importantly, the ordinary people of Valencia will not abandon their national poet. Grassroots neighbourhood associations have collectively designated his birthday as a date of popular celebration after the fashion of a Burns' Night. And it is precisely this constituency, along with the cultural agencies of the Catalan government in Barcelona, that have enabled due recognition of the centennial of, in the opinion of many, the finest poet to have emerged from Valencia since the medieval period.

Hotel Paris (HP)

Although the present collection was not published until 1973, its text was drafted in the middle 1950s as part of a trilogy formed by *El monòleg* (The Monologue) and *Testimoni d'Horaci* (Horatio Bears Witness), which would eventually appear in 1981. The hotel is an unusual location for lyrical deliberation and Hospitality Studies can offer some insight into the expectations that might be aroused in the modern reader by this choice. Indeed the very title of Caroline Field Levander and Matthew Pratt Guterl's monograph, *Hotel Life: The Story of a Place Where Anything Can Happen* (2015), indicates the latency of the setting. Our first impression is that these residences, "both a hiatus and a haven—a space in which the market-weary laborer can seek solace, comfort, and new beginnings" (2015, 69), are associated with rebirth and regeneration. For Robbie Moore they were "a testing ground for a transformation in gender relations, in the mobility and independence of women, in the political organisation of suffrage campaigns, and the loosening of the institutions of marriage and the family." (2021, 17)

However, as all movie fans and admirers of Edward Hopper know, there is also an inevitably sinister dimension attached to the institution. As both temporary and coldly familiar accommodation—and the frequent sites for suicide—, these premises are particularly suited for the psychological thriller, horror and disaster genre as exemplified by *Psycho* (Hitchcock, 1960), *The Shining* (Kubrick, 1980) and *The Towering Inferno* (Guillermin, 1974). The morose and alienating atmosphere of such popular ballads as *Heartbreak Hotel* (Axton & Durden, 1956) and *Hotel California* (Felder, Hendon & Frey, 1977) underline this experience. And it is precisely this morbid quality and its deathly stasis that Estellés will exploit in direct contrast to the previously mentioned positive expectations aroused by the hotel, particularly with respect to the female condition.

In general, the critical reaction to the collection has been excellent and has married this ambience to appropriate theoretical deliberation on the theme of location. The chronotope, advanced by Mikhail Bakhtin, is a case in point and defined by *The Oxford Dictionary of Literary Terms* (2015) as an attempt "to refer to the co-ordinates of time and space invoked by a given narrative; in other words, to the 'setting', considered as a spatio-temporal whole." Viewed in this way, the evocation of the eponymous hotel observed by Estellés on his trip to Barcelona in 1956 will offer a vision of the life experience in Catalonia during the period when the Dictatorship was at its strongest. (Carbó 2014, 44)

The lyrical snapshot provided is, in fact, painfully accurate and privileges an insight into the female condition in Franco's autocracy. Unlike the novels of James, however, attention does not focus on the possible empowerment of women among the privileged ranks of the bourgeoisie but on females in general who may be regarded as the most disadvantaged constituency under Spain's phallocracy. Even the widow of Ovidi in XXI, the most comfortably off representative of her sex, is pictured in a parlous light. Though in receipt of a pension — a benefit generally denied to those who had supported the Republican cause — and, enjoying a daily meeting in the café with her group of friends, her comfort is slight due to the frugality of her income. And to keep up the appearance of being well-off, she deftly consumes crumbs of bread which she filches from a crust "discreetly hidden in her pocket."

Moreover, the mindless repetition of her mantra, "My dear departed Ovidi... God keep him in his glory", reveals not only a Francoist wife's total dependence on her husband but also the obligatory, unquestioning adherence to the repressive monogamous ethics of national-catholicism, the crudely enforced religious regime of the directorate. The contradictory representation of her Ovidi—as short and tall, fat and thin, happy and sad, —posits the husband, even when deceased, as an everyman—"not a name but the world"—to whom the subservience of the devoted wife is total and obligatory.

More precarious, however, was the situation of the masses of women on the losing side of the Civil War. With their menfolk dead, imprisoned or ostracised, these wives and mothers had to go to extremes to put food on the table. Poem VII offers a sorry list of the multiple jobs which they were obliged to take—a common practice given the poverty of the period and known as *pluriempleo*—, often leaving children at home and unsupervised: from lavatory assistant, cleaner or seamstress, hawker of odds and ends to the more desperate function of sex worker or bordello madam. The identification of the hotel with prostitution— with rooms "for rent by the hour"— appears starkly in the first poem and pervades the work. And woman as brutalised victim is exposed likewise in XVII as she suffers "obscure revenge with an endless welter of blows." Indeed, the previous poem wherein the "poor, defenceless bodies" of females are subject inevitably to the savage partiality of a preordained order of *machismo*, established a desperate equation: that, just like physics, this national-catholic environment had its own "natural" laws of violent female subjugation. Needless to say, the conversion of wife-battering into a lyrical theme is a bold and original practice in the Europe of the mid 1950s.

Once again in this context of time and space, critics have successfully adduced Michel Foucault's speculation on heterotopia, particularly from the perspective of the hotel as a site of deviation, in its condition as both a private and public institution. In Franco's Spain, of course, extramarital sex was taboo. However, in order not to compromise the whims and desires of wealthy stalwarts of the regime who revelled in such "deviance", the dive hotel could act as cover for their promiscuity and so accommodate their rule breaking. The practice is brilliantly exposed in Carles Balagué's documentary on a notorious Barcelona brothel of the time, *La casita blanca, la ciudad oculta* (2002). What is clear in both cases, however, is that the hierarchy patent in these "emplacements" mirrors the callous brutality of the dictatorship's sexist machinery which might otherwise be swept under the carpet and lie hidden beneath the surface. Indeed, in IV, the poet reveals that his motive for writing is precisely to denounce these "affairs to be kept silent (…) the sputum of the sperm." Or, as he reiterates in IX:

> However, write I must in the biggest book of all
> and in the roundest hand both tiny and incisive
> while some poor young girl takes a bite out of a blanket,
> while some poor young widow wipes it clean in a bidet.

In fact, a series of motifs combine to enhance the censure. The figure of the virgin about to be coerced (I, IX, XV) crystallises, in her panic, the brutal control of a system which, by the denial of any alternative, forces her into sexual obeisance. The metal bed (I, V) evokes, in turn, the austere, clinical nature of the exercise of authority on the part of the empowered male. Furnishings of this type are to be found in the related heterotopia of hospitals and prisons which accentuates the notions of solitude, confinement, disease and criminalisation implicit in prostitution.

Julia Kristeva's (1982) meditation on abjection has also been successfully cited in the relation to the theme of corruption. Herein, decomposition—especially in terms of the cadaver and waste products—, abounds: the Morgue (III); death intuited in the dust under the table (III, X); sin, decay and corpses sketched between toilet and bidet (IV, IX); birth, death, deflowerment, adultery and masturbation—each with their associated fluids—, are imagined as present in the self-same bed in XV. Kristeva argues that, despite the immediate reaction of horror and repulsion provoked by such references, the morbid fascination with excreta and related matter represents a breaking down of borders between subject and the other which compromises identity, system and order.

The accompanying collapse in ethics and jurisprudence reflects the dystopia of dictatorship as described in HP. In this way, corruption—in all senses of the word—is posited as the hallmark of the regime. What is also patent, of course, is the anonymity general to the experience. The only identification allowed in this context is the ironic nomenclature of the hotel—whose reality is the antithesis of the romance, elegance and magnificence evoked by the French capital— and reference to Françoise (and tangentially to Hildegarde), the sex workers. Otherwise, the motif of the abject enhances the lack of definition and identity which typifies the guests and, by extension, the Catalan nation whose institutions, language and culture had all been disappeared by the homogeneity of the Francoist diktat. All these constituencies are coldly entangled by the narrator into a web of interrelations which anticipates the "networked" subjectivity, outlined by Maud Ellman, which reduces "the human subject to a knot or intersection, rather than an independent agent, in the webs of communication, commodities and capital." (Moore 2021, 3)

Performance and Artifice

The caustic censure of the system, however, should not distract from the sophistication of the verse as Estellés compounds his social critique with a no less imaginative experiment in narrative. If hotels blur the distinction between interior and exterior, public and private, the opening lines dwell precisely on this ambiguity:

> The plough is there, yellowish, a yellowness of bone,
> the cranium of the ass amid the tender brushwood.
> There is a background of sheets, hanging out to dry:

> there is a boat on the sands and other things, Françoise.
> There are footprints too, serious and all spaced out;
> there is the outline of two buttocks, cheerful and small,
> and loneliness, Françoise, and more loneliness still.

Rather than a mere description of the port exterior to the hotel, this scene described and its "background" could also be an ekphrastic reference to a painting. The insistent yellowness, eroticism and ass's skull recall specifically the jaundiced landscapes of Franco's favourite and self-proclaimed "universal" Catalan, Salvador Dalí. The tone of the discourse is flat and aseptic, reading something like a stage direction. The insistent and non-committal "there is" or "there are", for example, is repeated 57 times in 23 poems and becomes reminiscent of the detail of a screenplay.

Indeed, a cinematic dimension pervades the collection: hardly surprising in the work of a film addict like Estellés. In III, the term svengali relates to the eponymous film of 1954 directed by Donald Wolfit where Hildegarde (Kneff), named twice in the poem, stars as leading lady. Here the protagonist Trilby is controlled by David Kossof's mesmeric arch-villain, losing all resolve and control of her actions, which also mirrors the male power over women in Franco's phallocracy. A similar fictional dimension, however, surrounds the Swiss girl and her cousin in the final poem. The couple, "brutally" asleep after a menacing sequence of pursuit with candelabra, end up immolated in a blazing flat. The hyperbole of this terror-filled denouement is underscored in the verse by the painfully anaphoric polysindeton. Indeed, both setting and stage furniture bear all the markings of the horror genre, especially the crypt where "the noble knights lie buried" and the cataleptic siblings who perish in this manner in *The Fall of the House of Usher*, both in Epstein's silent classic of 1928 or Ivan Barnett's 1950 remake.

Levander and Guterl sum up, appropriately for our context, the suitability of the hotel as stage for such performative excess: "so ubiquitous is death in a hotel that it can at times feel staged, a bit melodramatic." (87) And in XV, the script of the life cycle from gestation to mortuary is so in-keeping with the cold hyperbole of the horror genre that the lines might easily be recited with the sinister timbre of Vincent Price or Peter Lorre.

> Perhaps somebody died in the bed where I lie (…)
> Perhaps some other night a woman gave birth
> a babe began to cry, a virgin's scream rang out,
> an act of adultery, as it is known, was committed.
> Perhaps in this very bed an infant was found dead.

The dramatic dimension, of course, emphasises artificiality particularly in deportment or role playing. In fact, the "catalogue" that the poet is preparing in IX refers precisely to the mindless repetition in the lives of the residents who make up a cast of secondary characters, with anaphora underscoring the bland anonymity of the experience:

> There is the guest who died, no one knows where he is from
> and the guest who expects a telegramme delivered,
> the guest who lends an ear to marital sexual union,
> there is the well-mannered guest who has a word for no one.

Indeed, the lack of identity and authenticity is attributable to the narrator himself whose failing becomes particularly evident in XI. For all his denunciation of prostitution as an exercise in brutal exploitation and moral turpitude, he offers precious little in terms of resistance. In fact, any effort to fight against this iniquity is replaced by self-pity and a recidivist desire to conform, crystallised by the employment of religious terminology to describe what had been previously condemned as a social malaise.

> A feeling of failure deep down inside your bones,
> the infantile desire to be a child and good,
> completely to love some anonymous whore (…)
> To be tender with her, obsequious and noble (…)
> Living in complete and persistent failure, Françoise.

What is witnessed here is the obfuscation by the narrator of a problem through recourse to evangelical naivity (Matthew 18, 2–5) and imitation of the discredited modes of Romantic deportment. The egocentric desire to save women from prostitution is a commonplace evident in pot boilers from *La Traviata* to *Pretty Woman* (Marshall, 1990). Such backsliding is continued in XIV when, despite a degree of emotional solidarity, the fundamental reaction to the contemplation of the sex worker's sensuous body is a regression to the same dyad of childlike resolve and repentance for national-catholic transgression: "I am moved by a desire to be completely good (…) and cry between your breasts, Françoise, and in your hair."

Implicit in this *décalage* between author and narrator is a censure particularly reminiscent of Sartre's existential deliberation which was hugely influential in the aftermath of World War II. In simple terms, the residents of this hotel exist merely in the category of *en soi*—a being in itself—, which is summarised by *The Oxford Dictionary of Philosophy* (2008) as "the self-sufficient, lumpy, contingent being of ordinary things." Like inanimate objects they are "a definable and complete essence yet are not conscious of themselves or their essential completeness." The experience is described appropriately in XI: "to lie waiting and waiting like stone, nothing more".

Accordingly, the ritual of the imagined daily phone call in XVIII would be dismissed by Sartre as an example of *mauvaise foi* which *A Dictionary of Critical Theory* (2018) defines as a lie to oneself: "a form of self-deception and avoidance of one's freedom" which accounts for "the inauthenticity inherent in modern life: the individual subject's failure to grasp the truth of their situation in late capitalism." Here the guest performs a daily pantomime of going down to reception to ask if anyone has phoned to leave a message. The sequence is choreographed in a display of Noel Coward proportions with the individual adopting "the noblest of poses" as he enquires in a "falsely negligent tone." The resident knows full well, however, that no call has been, or will ever be, received for him. Yet rather than confront the reality of his situation and exploit through analysis the opportunity for freedom of the purposive *pour soi*, he prefers to indulge completely in a display of ostentation, consuming himself totally in this performance.

Just like Sartre's example of the waiter, this individual devotes himself completely to escapist strategies which sidetrack from him from any objective of significance. The same, indeed, can be said of the narrator. Despite his insistent, sardonic denunciation of female exploitation, particularly the case of prostitution, instead of attempting to find means to resist this social malaise he regresses into childhood, feeling the urge to cry on his substitute mother's breast. A rare moment of self-analysis in XX which, with its "promises that are made, promises unfulfilled", admits the lack of purpose to this existence is illustrated in the previous poem by the fixation with the tram.

Modes of transport are frequently employed in literature and the arts as a means of escape to new worlds and experiences. In XIX, however, there is merely the unthinking repetition of the tram's movement which, having advanced on its tracks, returns ceaselessly to its point of origin. It is precisely in this context that the nonchalant reference to death may be understood. The frequent juxtaposition of the dead guest with other corpses and cadavers reflects, in terms of existentialism, the lack of qualitative difference between life and death in the case of the residents. The *en soi* experience is satirised to such an extent that the dead inmate in XIII remains unaware of his changed state; and even the pathologist is unsure whether there has been any significant modification in his condition:

> He remains unaware, so noble, so very noble
> his body still appears. The pathologist halts
> a moment, looks at it and, gazing at the assistants,
> he pinches at an armpit and asks ever so slowly:
> "Gentlemen, are you sure we are dealing with the dead?"

Given the complete lack of existential awareness among this group, it is ironic that the possibility for personal renewal should be habitually associated with the hotel which is "a kind of seductive portal or doorway into new modes of self-making but also as a kind of doorstop or holding pen, encouraging the disoriented, anxious, and perpetual traveller through space to take advantage of a momentary respite." (Field Levander & Pratt Guterl 2015, 70) There again, the holding pen is, of course, reminiscent of the drawing room location in Sartre's *Huis clos* (1964) and, in our collection, death similarly implies no sense of release just bland continuity underlined by "the hotel's affinity with other modern despair-inducing institutions like the prison, for the prison along with the hotel is a locus for hopelessness and, all too frequently, final endings." (Field Levander & Pratt Guterl 2015, 97) The last line of the collection, depicting a skull trundling down a flight of stairs, provides an apt evocation of this experience.

In order to assess our author's creation in the context of contemporary Europe, it might prove fruitful to conclude by briefly comparing and contrasting HP with other thematically related offerings. Alain Resnais' new wave film *L'Année dernière à Marienbad* (1961), for example, is also set in a hotel though the palatial Schloss Nymphenburg of Bavaria, with its luxurious topiary gardens, might appear completely removed from a seedy Barcelona boarding house. Despite the variance in the location and social class—from Catalan lumpenproletariat to French haute bourgeoisie—there is a clear similarity in structure and theme.

In the picture, as in the verse, the narrator is a participant in the action. And his insistent voice over, a largely one-sided dialogue with the leading lady, is identical in tone, authority and apparent nonchalance. The movie's monochrome complements the austerity of the verse; and the intentionally laboured repetition of set pieces in the screenplay reflects the exaggerated recourse to anaphora in the poetry. These strategies serve to illustrate the *en soi* existence of both sets of guests and the unending sameness of the experience. Their shallow homogeneity is enhanced by anonymity: Estellés's residents have no names while the French protagonists are mere letters—X, A and M. The love triangle, in which the latter are apparently involved, is so insignificant that Delphine Seyrig spends the whole film trying to remember if she really took part in the affair even though it occurred only "last year".

If the superficiality of Estellés's guests is registered through a daily ritual of pantomime, the excessive verbal and graphic attention paid to the intricacy of the baroque artistry on walls, ceilings and carpeted floors of the palace mirrors the same lack of substance and depth. The automatism is accentuated as characters are shot as immobile mannikins, frequently beside stone statues in the grounds as the camera, the only element which moves with any decision, sweeps over them, leaving them motionlessly adrift. Indeed, pure stasis surrounds on-stage actors and audience in the *mise en abyme* of the play. And the ekphrasis of the Dalinian painting, which we suggest is the *point de départ* of the poem, is recalled by a similar pastiche of individuals frozen in the topiary gardens. Here, as in Dalí's oeuvre, the only sense of time passing in any significant sense is registered by the angle and elongation of the shadows cast. Needless to say, in terms of ethos, language and stark censure of the bourgeoisie the film is highly reminiscent of such Buñuelian classics as *L'Age d'or* (1930) and *El ángel exterminador* (1962).

In terms of the meditation on the theme of national minorities, in *Under Milk Wood* (1956) Dylan Thomas frames a village rather than a hotel as metonym for his nation.[2] In Estellés's case, Francoist political and cultural thuggery had, of course, completely "disappeared" all vestiges of Catalan national difference from the homogenised state. A victim of such repression was the Valencian himself whose publications were sidelined by censorship and the machinery of state for almost a generation. As a result, in our text and others from the 1950s, there is not the slightest reference to or apology for collective difference. Indeed, the uninterrupted monologue of the trilogy underlines the connection between dictator and dictation. In this context, all concerned have been coerced into total subservience, a solipsistic acquiesence exemplified by the teenager in XV who, devoid of hope of any meaningful fulfillment, uses his room to offer "homage to Onan."

Thomas's masterpiece may, like HP, be set on the marine periphery. However, the slave labour of Franco's industrial metropolis gives way to diversity and spontaneity in the Welsh seaside village. Though caricatures of village types, their colloquial vitality rescues them from the monotone and drudgery of their anonymous counterparts. The town may be a "backwater of life" but its natives possess "a salty individuality of their own" as evidenced by the large cast's uninvited intrusions which punctuate the voice-over narrative. Their chorus

---

2 The version referenced of Thomas's dramatic poem is that of Project Gutenburg Australia which includes no page numbers: https://gutenberg.net.au/ebooks06/0608221h.html.

of countless interruptions is clearly designed to evoke the empowerment of democracy.

What is more, the melodic intonation of the inhabitants, so typical of the Principality, adds weight and charge to the appreciation of the differential fact of this national minority as is crystallised by the treacle-rich diction of Richard Burton's narration in the versions of both radio (1954) and film (Sinclair, 1972). The staccato toponymy chanted by vicar and would-be druid Eli Jenkins underlines the autochthony: "By Sawdde, Senny, Dovey, Dee,/ Edw, Eden, Aled, all,/ Taff and Towy broad and free,/ Llyfnant with its waterfall,/ Claerwen, Cleddau, Dulais, Daw,/ Ely, Gwili, Ogwr, Nedd,/ Small is our River Dewi, Lord,/ A baby on a rushy bed."

The alexandrine monotony of the Catalan texts is also replaced by the charged vitality of Dylan Thomas's explosive and idiosyncratic prosody. The overlay of enchantment in this seaside village emerges from an idiom whose surreal leaps exceed the boundaries of semantics, pointing to a rich variety of experience. The vivacity, imagination and humour weave a spell where death has no dominion, as depicted hilariously by twice-widowed Mrs Ogmore-Pritchard who shares a bed with the ghosts of her two late husbands; and the dead in the graveyard who form a "glee party" to welcome the spring under licentious vegetables that "make love" above them. In this way, a charged magical realism replaces the previous depiction of a forlorn existentialism.

That is not to say that the dramatic poem is not critical of local failings. The lack of any real significance to life in the village is exemplified by its mock-celtic name: Llareggub (read backwards!) The repression of the narrow, chapel mentality is evoked similarly by the description of the town as "starless and bible-black." The petty intolerance typical of such rural communities and their vindictive gossip—and charactered by spiteful Mrs Pugh and Mrs Ogden-Pritchard—is lampooned savagely in the character of Willy Nilly. The postman is so open with his intrusion into other people's business that, on their doorstep, he can recite verbatim the content of the letters he delivers so that none of the townsfolk actually bothers opening their correspondence.

An attempt at religious repression similar to that of HP may be evident in the "Thou Shalt Not" etched on the walls of the village houses, though its practice is no way criminal or prohibitive. Libidinal Mr Waldo may have his wife and mother shriek to him from beyond the grave, warning about the heinous crime of causing a scandal; but "drunk in the dusky wood" he still "hugs his lovely Polly Garter under the eyes and rattling tongues of the neighbours and the birds, and he does not care." Unlike their Catalan counterparts, the same sexual empowerment is afforded the women folk. Tyrannical gossip Mrs Pugh might want aptly named P.C. Attila Rees to arrest fecund Polly Garter for "having babies." The lyrical song of the unmarried mother of many, however, finds her rejoicing in her promiscuity with "Tom, Dick and Harry" and the "good bad boys from the farms."

Life in the village may be also banal, as with deceased Mr Ogmore who recites the chores his repressive wife imposes on him daily: "I must put my pyjamas in the drawer marked pyjamas." Indeed, the mark of his widow's narrow-mindedness is manifest in the everyday task she ascribes to her second deceased husband: "And before you let the sun in, mind it wipes its shoes!" These shortcomings, however, pale into insignificance. The surreal aesthetics, wit and intense spirituality of *Under Milk Wood* offer a triumphant vision of the vital permanence of the location and the nation it represents. Sadly, the experience of life in contemporary Catalonia can attest no such contestatory polyphony. And it is the dour monologue of moral, cultural and financial repression of Franco's autocracy that we are presented with in HP. It will not be until the next decade when, armed with the academic coherence of the radical, national thesis of Joan Fuster and inspired by the growth of mass Catalan consciousness in Valencia, Estellés will begin to employ similar strategies of artistry and invention as an apology for his nation.

Car l'amour et la mort n'est qu'une même chose.
Ronsard

E·l fan morir sense un punt de record...
Ausiàs March

–Ai, las! Industriós, em faç obscena.
J. V. Foix

Car l'amour et la mort n'est qu'une même chose.
Ronsard

And they put him to death, with no time to remember...
Ausiàs March

–Your diligence, alas!, doth render me obscene.
J. V. Foix

I

Hi ha l'aladre, groguenc, amb una grogor d'os,
i hi ha el crani de l'ase entre les brosses tendres
i hi ha una llunyania de llençols eixugant-se:
hi ha una barca en l'arena, hi ha altres coses, Françoise.
Hi ha petjades també, espaiades i greus,
hi ha el senyal d'unes natges alegres i petites,
i soledat, Françoise, més soledat encara.
Hi ha també el llit metàl·lic, hi ha l'habitació
per hores, hi ha la verge amb uns ulls grans pel pànic,
i nua, en un racó, mirant avançar l'home:
hi ha la virtut, Françoise, i la virginitat,
i l'hivern, a la platja, i hi ha els cristalls, tots bruts,
i hi ha els llençols greixosos, esgarrats amb les ungles,
i hi ha els vaixells, Françoise, amb noms prestigiosos,
en l'aigua lenta i trista i oliosa del port.
Hi ha dos vaixells danesos carregant mandarina.

Hotel Paris

I

The plough is there, yellowish, a yellowness of bone,
the cranium of the ass amid the tender brushwood.
There is a background of sheets, hanging out to dry:
there is a boat on the sands and other things, Françoise.
There are footprints too, serious and all spaced out;
there is the outline of two buttocks, cheerful and small,
and loneliness, Françoise, and more loneliness still.
There is the metal bed as well, there is the room
for rent by the hour and the virgin, in wide-eyed panic
and naked in a corner, watching the man draw near.
There is virtue, Françoise, there is virginity;
and winter on the beach, the window panes all dirty.
There are also soiled sheets, furrowed by fingernails,
and there are ships, Françoise, their names of real prestige,
on the slow and sad and oily water of the port.
Two Danish ships are loading mandarin oranges.

II

Hi ha encàrrecs, hi ha consignes, hi ha flames a trametre.
Ens cal dubtar també, i tenir fam i fred
i aguardar, sense son, tota la nit així,
fins que el dubte s'acabe, fins que la nit s'acabe.
Hi ha pecats, hi ha desgràcies, hi ha el dubte, la bandera.
De tot açò, gemecs, les mans apegaloses,
el crit sense resposta, el silenci, la fúria.

II

There are errands, orders, there are flames to consign.
We must hesitate as well, being hungry, being cold,
spending all the night waiting, without sleep, just like that,
till hesitation ends, till night draws to a close.
There are sins, misfortunes, there is doubt, there is the flag.
From all of this come groans, hands both moist and sticky,
The cry without reply, the silence, the fury.

III

I hi ha la mort, Françoise, i més coses encara.
Hi ha el record d'Hildegarde, per exemple, dempeus;
hi ha els deixebles amb bruses i hi ha la salamandra;
hi ha també els fulls de «cànson», i hi ha la boira en draps,
i hi ha l'aigua caent pels porxos, pels balcons.
Hi ha els muscles d'Hildegarde, les seues cuixes, llargues;
hi ha els seus pits, hi ha un penjat, hi ha la Morgue, hi ha tant.
Hi ha les ungles, Françoise, les ungles de Svengali.
L'enrenou de la pluja damunt les conilleres.

III

And there is death, Françoise, and other things as well.
There is the memory, say, of Hildegarde on her feet;
there are disciples with blouses, there is the salamander;
the sheets of Canson paper, there is fog in the cloths:
and there is water falling on balconies, on porches.
There are Hildegarde's shoulders, her never ending thighs;
there are her breasts, a hanged man, the Morgue, there is so much.
There are fingernails, Françoise, the long nails of Svengali.
The patter of the rain upon the rabbit hutches.

IV

De lentes persistències, d'afers silenciosos,
de les fruites que cauen dels carros i es podreixen;
com qui agafa amb les mans la cendra d'un cadàver
i desfent l'estatura del silenci i l'espera
fa un muntó qualsevol, vagament adorable.
He fet mal, cau el vespre darrere els cristalls bruts;
tots han sortit i són ara a les seues cases.
Jo dec seguir, encara, escrivint lentament,
no sé quantes vegades, unes úniques coses.
La tebior d'una aigua, els gargalls de l'esperma.

IV

Of slow persistencies, affairs to be kept silent,
of fruits which fall from carts rotting where they lie;
like to that man who grabs the ash from a cadaver
and undoing the stature of silence and the waiting
fashions an ordinary, vaguely adorable pile.
I have done wrong. The evening falls round dirty window panes.
Everyone has left: they are all back in their own homes.
I must press on slowly, withal, as I keep on writing,
over and over again, the same old same old things.
A water which is lukewarm, the sputum of the sperm.

V

Mire el llit, el meu llit, metàl·lic a l'hotel.
Té, Françoise, l'estatura exacta del pecat.
Considere els llençols i el cobertor, vermell,
i les parets verdoses i l'espill i el bidet,
i lleve el cobertor amb certa lentitud;
toque els llençols, humits, i blancs, i suavíssims.
Pense unes cuixes tendres, Françoise, pense un cos d'aigua.
Pense el pes del ruixim, Françoise, i pense l'ègloga.

V

I see the bed, my bed, metal in the hotel.
Its stature, Françoise, is exactly that of sin.
I consider its sheets and its red overblanket
and the green-hued walls, the mirror and the bidet;
I withdraw the blanket with a certain slowness.
I touch the humid sheets: they are white and so soft.
I think of tender thighs, Françoise, a body of water.
I think the weight of the spray, Françoise. I think the eclogue.

VI

Tornaria a parlar lentament d'Hildegarde;
parlaria, Françoise, del seu cos d'or cremat,
enumerant, Françoise, un per un, els seus béns,
demorant-me, Françoise, morint-me en cadascun.
El seu cos d'or cremat i el seu cos d'aigua esvelta,
i el seu cos forestal, i una lluna germànica.

VI

Once more would I speak slowly about Hildegarde.
I would speak, Françoise, of her body of burnt gold,
numbering, Françoise, its effects one by one
and dwelling, Françoise, dying on every one.
Her body of burnt gold and her body of lithe water,
her body of the forest, of a Germanic moon.

VII

La dona que ven coses, a la nit, a la porta
del bar, del cabaret; la dona que vigila
el wàter de les dones; la dona que ha deixat
la vaixella escurada i els tres fills en el llit
i va a fer certes coses, a la nit, vora el riu;
i la dona que va tenir un fill i no
sap d'ell des de la guerra, i resa a sant Antoni;
la dona que neteja el servei del cafè
i la dona que agrana les habitacions
del vell hotel per hores i parelles febrils;
i la dona que planxa, i la dona que cus,
i la dona que fa l'article de les dones,
i diu les excel·lències de cadascuna d'elles,
sospesant-los els pits, colpejant-los les natges
i entra després la safa i pondera les còpules;
i la dona que prega per la feina de l'home
i pel fill i la filla; i la dona que va
tenir un primer nuvi; i la dona que vol
tenir un fill, quedar aquesta nit prenyada.

VII

The woman selling things at night outside the door
of the bar, of the night-spot; the woman looking after
the ladies convenience; the woman who has left
the dishes washed and dried and her three kids in bed
off to do this and that, at night, down by the river;
and the woman who had a boy but now knows nothing
about him since the war but prays to Saint Anthony;
the woman who cleans the toilets in the café and
the woman pushing broom, who is paid by the hour,
in the old hotel rooms and the febrile couples;
and the woman who irons and the woman who sews,
and the woman with the sales pitch for the women
and sings out the praises of each and every one,
running the rule over their breasts, slapping them on the buttocks,
then fetches in the basin, musing on copulation;
and the woman who prays for her man to find work
and for their son and daughter; and the woman who once
had a first boy-friend; and the woman who wants
to have a child, to get pregnant that very night.

VIII

El principi i la fi són la mateixa cosa.
Són un poble, Françoise, on viuen els meus pares,
on vaig nàixer i vaig fer els primers pecats,
on torne cada dia, inesperadament,
mentre vaig, vinc i torne entre les meues coses.
El principi i la fi són un poble, Françoise.

VIII

The beginning and the end are both the same thing.
They are a village, Françoise, where my parents live,
where I too was born and committed my first sins;
where each day I return, unexpectedly,
while I come and go and come again with my things.
The beginning and the end are a village, Françoise.

IX

Vaig fent el trist catàleg, el meu nocturn catàleg
d'estupres, d'adulteris, de violacions,
entre el cruixir dels llits i el cruixir dels taüts,
l'enrenou de la ploma sobre el paper grossíssim,
i l'enrenou dels plats, les culleres, els wàters,
els cadàvers que hi ha desfent-se en la bodega.
Hi ha l'hoste que s'ha mort i no se sap d'on és,
i hi ha l'hoste que espera que arribe un telegrama,
com hi ha l'hoste que escolta el coit d'un matrimoni
i hi ha l'hoste, cortès, que no parla amb ningú.
Però jo dec escriure, en el llibre més gran
i amb la lletra més clara, petita i incisiva,
mentre una pobra jove mossega un cobertor,
mentre una pobra vídua s'ho renta en un bidet,
mentre el pobre poeta escriu versos indignes,
mentre al pobre home ric li ve un dolor d'estómac,
mentre les pobres gents van fent les pobres coses
i el captaire es pessiga tendrament les lladelles,
humils, d'una color de mel delicadíssima,
i amablement les deixa en la seua mà oberta.

IX

I am drafting a sad catalogue, my catalogue of the night,
of stuprums, of adulteries, of rapes, of violations,
amid groaning of beds and the groaning of coffins,
the scratching of my pen on this rankest of paper,
the clanking of plates, of spoons, of toilet bowls,
the corpses decomposing in the cellar below.
There is the guest who died, no one knows where he is from
and the guest who expects a telegramme delivered,
the guest who lends an ear to marital sexual union,
there is the well-mannered guest who has a word for no one.
However, write I must in the biggest book of all
and in the roundest hand both tiny and incisive
while some poor young girl takes a bite out of a blanket,
while some poor young widow wipes it clean in a bidet,
while some poor young poet pens unbefitting lines,
while the poor rich man is beset by tummy ache,
while the poor folk get on with their poor old business
and the beggar squeezes tenderly his crab lice,
lowly but of a most delicate honeyed hue,
and leaves them lovingly in the palm of his open hand.

X

La mort creix i prospera, misteriosament,
com la pols, amb la pols domèstica, Françoise,
que s'hi va acumulant dessota cada pota
de la taula, Françoise, una pols, unes coses,
semblant aquelles coses que s'hi fan al melic,
dessota cada pota de la taula, del llit,
en els plecs del melic, una pols, unes coses.

X

Death grows and prospers, quite mysteriously,
like dust with dust around the house, Françoise,
which grows and grows and grows under every single leg
of the table, Françoise, dust and bits and bobs,
like little balls of fluff that gather in your navel,
under each leg of the table, or each leg of the bed,
in the tucks of your navel, dust and bits and bobs.

XI

El cap-al-tard urbà, els llums a les finestres,
una humitat, un lent desig només de jaure,
d'esperar com la pedra, i només esperar,
una sensació de fracàs dins els ossos,
el desig pueril d'ésser infant i bo,
d'amar, completament, alguna puta anònima,
alguna puta efímera que no constarà en acta,
i ser amb ella tendre i obsequiós i noble,
i veure-la dubtar de tot el que ella pensa,
amb un llum instantani, d'estupor, en els ulls,
i agafar-la del braç i passejar, en calma,
mirant aparadors, i jaure pobrament,
i jaure tristament, tenir fred i atansar-nos.
De persistir, del tot, en el fracàs, Françoise.

XI

Evening in the city with lights on in the windows,
dampness and slow desire solely to rest in peace,
to lie waiting and waiting like stone, nothing more,
a feeling of failure deep down inside your bones,
the infantile desire to be a child and good,
completely to love some anonymous whore,
some ephemeral whore not featuring in the minutes,
to be tender with her, obsequious and noble
and to watch her question everything she believes,
with a sparkle of light, of stupor, in her eyes
and take her by the arm strolling calmly about
and go off window shopping, then rest poorly in peace
and rest sadly in peace, being cold drawing close.
Living in complete and persistent failure, Françoise.

XII

Era un poble petit, humil i blanc de calç,
amb uns pins i una sèquia i unes pedres antigues
i un cel tibant, i es veia la mar damunt els arbres,
i pel vespre volaven els coloms. Era un poble
humil, amb carrers amples, i corrals, i balcons,
i el tren creuant les hortes, i una senzilla fe.

XII

It was a tiny village, lowly and white as lime,
with pine-trees and a conduit and stones from ancient times,
a brittle sky, over the trees you saw the sea;
in the evening doves would fly. It was a lowly village.
Its streets were wide and with corrals and balconies,
trains crossing the market gardens: a simple faith.

XIII

Hi ha l'hoste que s'ha mort i no se n'ha adonat,
i això que aquella mort, la seua, és personal
i, més, intransferible, segons els documents,
i que el trauen del llit i el duen al Dipòsit,
i no se n'assabenta, i el despullen i el deixen
damunt el marbre blanc, i el renten, i li fan
certes coses, aquells tràmits que s'han de fer,
i no se n'assabenta, de digne, de digníssim
que és encara el seu cos, i el forense es detura
un moment, el contempla i mira els practicants
i es pessiga una aixella i lentament pregunta:
«Senyors, esteu segurs que tractem amb un mort?»

XIII

There is the guest who has died yet has not realised
despite the fact this death, his own, is personal
and non-transferable as documents confirm.
They lift him out of bed and take him to the Morgue
without him noticing. He is undressed and left
on a white marble slab. He is washed and certain things
are done to him in line with normal practice and such.
He remains unaware, so noble, so very noble
his body still appears. The pathologist halts
a moment, looks at it and, gazing at the assistants,
he pinches at an armpit and asks ever so slowly:
"Gentlemen, are you sure we are dealing with the dead?"

XIV

En veure't escampada per sobre el llit, Françoise,
amb les mans enllaçades darrere el tòs dolcíssim,
m'entra el desig, Françoise, d'ésser bo totalment,
i m'entren unes ganes terribles de plorar,
plorar entre els teus pits, Françoise, i els teus cabells,
i de dir-te germana, car el pecat, Françoise,
hi ha certs moments que ajunta com no ajunta la sang.
El pecat, el fracàs, totes aquestes coses.

XIV

As I see you stretched out across the bed, Françoise,
your hands entwined beneath the sweetness of your neck,
I am moved by a desire to be completely good.
I feel a dreadful urge to just break down in tears
and cry between your breasts, Françoise, and in your hair
and to call you my sister; for sin has certain moments,
Françoise, that bind much more than blood can bind.
Wrongdoing, failure and other things like these.

XV

Potser ha mort algú en el llit on em gite,
potser aquests llençols varen embolcallar,
de moment, algun mort, un pobre mort incògnit,
mentre se'n feia càrrec el Jutjat del seu cos;
potser ha mort algú que venia a resoldre
un assumpte, unes coses: algú ha mort, sense dubte,
en el llit on em gite, una nit qualsevulla,
lluny de la seua casa, del seu poble, dels seus,
del corral i els geranis, de l'esposa, dels pares.
Algun adolescent ha dedicat a Onan,
de genolls en el llit, el seu càntic febril.
Algú no s'ha gitat, passetjant per l'estança
preocupat, fumant, despert tota la nit.
Potser, alguna nit, ha parit una dona,
ha plorat un infant, ha cridat una verge,
s'ha perpetrat allò que en diuen adulteri.
Potser, en aquest llit, va morir un infant.

XV

Perhaps somebody died in the bed where I lie.
Perhaps these very sheets were used, just for a moment,
to swaddle the deceased—a corpse, poor and unknown—,
until the coroner took charge of the cadaver;
perhaps that dead somebody had come here to sort out
some business or other: somebody died for sure
in the bed where I lie, on some or other night,
far away from their home, from their town, from their folks,
their garden and geraniums, from their spouse and their parents.
Some teenager or other paid homage to Onan
kneeling down on the bed in a febrile song of praise.
Somebody stayed up late, pacing around the room
smoking, preoccupied, awake the whole night long.
Perhaps some other night a woman gave birth,
a babe began to cry, a virgin's scream rang out,
an act of adultery, as it is known, was committed.
Perhaps in this very bed an infant was found dead.

XVI

Hi ha una electricitat, com hi ha uns requeriments
a un ordre, hi ha unes clàusules vigents i inabatibles,
com hi ha espases llarguíssimes i hi ha cossos inermes,
causes indefensables, i hi ha plaers només,
com hi ha el goig, absolut, que encara es perpetua
i hi ha els actes que moren ràpidament on naixen,
com hi ha un cel i un infern dirimint tots els plets.

XVI

There is electricity, just like there are requirements
for any order; and there are clauses, current and inflexible,
just like swords with long blades and poor, defenceless bodies:
indefensible actions and pleasures pure and simple,
like absolute delight, which lives on still, eternal;
and there are acts that die as quickly as they are born,
like there is a heaven and hell judging every action.

XVII

L'amant, feroç, que es venja en una amant atònita,
absurda, amb l'estupor en els ulls i en els llavis,
dreta, contra una tàpia; un amant venjatiu
de mai no se sabrà quina remota cosa,
l'enamorat discret que un dia, ancestralment,
necessita una víctima, una víctima estúpida,
i es venja obscurament, a grapats i trompades,
brutalment insistint, destrossant, miserable,
i amb la sang que així vessa entre unes cuixes té
un fulgor instantani de selva i dalt la lluna.

XVII

The lover who wreaks ferocious vengeance on his lady,
astonished, with stupor in her eyes and on her lips,
upright against a wall; a lover made vengeful
for a reason so remote it never will be known:
that most discreet of lovers who ancestrally one day
decides he needs a victim, any old stupid victim,
and wreaks obscure revenge with an endless welter of blows,
so brutally insistent and wretchedly destructive;
and with the blood he sheds between two thighs has thus
an instantaneous glimmer of forest and moon above.

XVIII

Veig l'hoste, l'hoste aquell que tots els cap-al-tards
baixa, greu, per l'escala, amb un posat digníssim,
ben vestit, i s'acosta, lentament, al *comptoir*
i pregunta, en un to falsament negligent
si li han telefonat aquell dia. Li diuen:
«No, senyor». I murmura: «És estrany». I se'n va,
però es gira i s'acosta novament, i encarrega:
«Si em telefonen, diga… No. Que em criden després».
Un dia qualsevol dels que té el calendari
li telefonaran i ell estarà dormint
a l'habitació i se n'haurà d'anar
de qualsevol manera, embolcallat, potser,
només amb un llençol. Baixarà per l'escala,
els peus per endavant, sobre els muscles de quatre,
i no preguntarà si li han telefonat:
i, qui ho sap, el silenci funeral d'aleshores
potser —potser— el trenque el timbre del telèfon.

XVIII

I see the guest, that guest who every single evening
comes seriously downstairs, with the noblest of poses,
well-dressed; and drawing slowly near to the *comptoir*
stops to enquire in a falsely negligent tone
if anyone has phoned that day for him. He is told:
"No, sir". And he mutters, "How very strange" and goes;
but he turns around and, drawing near once more, he barks:
"If someone calls then say…No: tell them to call back."
Then, one particular day—the same as any other—
a call will come for him and he will be fast asleep
stretched out up in his room; and he will have to come down
any old way he can—even swaddled perhaps
in a winding sheet. He will come down the stairs
feet first, carried on the shoulders of six stout men
and he will not enquire if anyone has called:
and, who knows?, the funereal silence of that moment
might just, perhaps, be broken by the ringing of a phone.

XIX

Els tramvies que duen les gents amunt i avall
i els tramvies que duen el taüt de l'albat
i els tramvies que duen gents alegres i tristes
i els tramvies que duen un nen entre les rodes
i els tramvies que duen la xicona de verd
i els tramvies que duen una dona plorant
i els tramvies que duen les gents a l'oficina
i els tramvies que duen les corones de flors
i els tramvies que duen els homosexuals
i els tramvies que duen una dona prenyada
i els tramvies que duen la puta amb ulls de son
i els tramvies que duen un home sense feina
i els tramvies que duen un condemnat a mort
i els tramvies que duen en Joan Maragall
i els tramvies que duen el manyà del cantó
i els tramvies que duen el rector de les monges
i els tramvies que venen i els tramvies que van
i un nen entre les rodes i uns bolquers plens de sang
i aquell orb que venia «Iguales para hoy...»

XIX

Streetcars that carry people up and down
and streetcars that carry a wee toddler's coffin
and streetcars that carry folks both happy and sad
and streetcars that carry away a kiddie under their wheels
and streetcars that carry the young lass in green
and streetcars that carry a woman in tears
and streetcars that carry folk off to the office
and streetcars that carry wreaths of flowers for funerals
and streetcars that carry along homosexuals
and streetcars that carry a woman with child
and streetcars that carry the sleepy-eyed hooker
and streetcars that carry a man out of work
and streetcars that carry a man condemned to death
and streetcars that carry poet Joan Maragall
and streetcars that carry the locksmith on the corner
and streetcars that carry the priest to the convent
and streetcars that come and streetcars that go
and a kiddie under their wheels and nappies stained with blood
and that man, partially sighted, selling lottery for today.

XX

Penediments a penes, confessions mal fetes,
les treves que es demanen i les treves que es prenen,
les promeses que es fan i que no s'acompleixen,
les coses que es demanen i el do que s'ha oblidat,
potser la confiança o potser l'esperança,
requeriments diaris, sol·licitacions,
els fervors instantanis, els pànics, els oblits.

XX

Repentance only just, confessions badly made,
truces that are requested, truces that are taken,
promises that are made, promises unfulfilled,
presents that are asked for, the gift that lies forgotten,
confidence perhaps or only hope perhaps,
the favours and requests of every single day,
the instantaneous fervours, the panics and things forgotten.

XXI

Cobra una pensió. Tots els dies de l'any
té, també, una tertúlia en un cafè. Conversa.
I diu: «El meu difunt Ovidi, en glòria estiga…»
Hi ha una amiga que té formiguer en un peu;
ella mai no ha tingut formiguer, però, en canvi,
«El meu difunt Ovidi…» El seu difunt Ovidi
era baix i era alt, era gros i era prim,
era trist i era alegre, segons allò que es parle.
No és un nom: és un món. No és un home, és el món.
«El meu difunt Ovidi, Déu el tinga en la glòria…»
Era bròfec i amable, era sempre fidel
i ho feia amb la veïna de l'entresol esquerra.
Lentament, mentrestant es parla, es diuen coses,
ella va pessigant molles d'un tros de pa
que duu discretament ocult a la butxaca.
«El meu difunt Ovidi, Déu el tinga en la glòria…»

XXI

She is paid a pension. Every day of the year,
she also meets up with friends in a café and says:
"My dear departed Ovidi, God rest his soul…"
A friend of hers has pins and needles in her foot;
she herself has never had pins and needles unlike
"My dear departed Ovidi…" Her dear departed Ovidi
was short and he was tall, he was fat and he was thin,
he was happy and he was sad, depending on the case.
Not a name but a world. Not a man but the world.
"My dear departed Ovidi, God keep in in his glory…"
He was loving and harsh and faithful to the end;
and knocking off the neighbour on the mezzanine.
Slowly as they speak, as things are being said,
she starts picking out crumbs from a slice of bread
that she carries discreetly hidden in her pocket.
"My dear departed Ovidi, God keep in in his glory…"

XXII

Com hi ha el fill sense els pares i els pares sense el fill
i xiques, al cinema, amb les cames obertes
i una mà entre les cuixes, i el rosari en família,
i hi ha el peó que es mata caent des d'un andami
i l'home que fa el pa i hi ha qui porta un metre
per saber el tamany escaient del taüt
i com hi ha els tramviaris que treballen la nit
de cap d'any i els forats de les piques i hi ha
l'ascensor amb un llum brut groguenc esperant
mentrestant la portera s'emborratxa de vi
i pixa per l'escala i la filla té por
i el marit està fent-ho amb la dona del metge
i els tramvies terribles amb l'enrenou dels ferros
i el metge que es dedica a trencar les anous
mentrestant la portera va pixant per l'escala
i trucant a les portes amb un colp de mamella
i el fill de la de l'arpa que s'ha mort fa tres dies
plora i plora i encén un ciri i posa el ciri
a l'ampolla del vi i contempla la Loren
i llavors la suïssa crida pel passadís
i el cosí la segueix brandant el canelobre
i la xica que es gita més aviat que mai
i un fred com una mà li puja per les cuixes
i hi ha un instant que pensa que té el cul més petit
i els veïns que s'han mort els dos intoxicats
l'altre dia i la dona i la filla no tenen
ganes de menjar res i ploren com les rates
i el cosí i la suïssa que dormen brutalment
i el canelobre encès i el cobertor encès
les cortines enceses i tot el pis encès
els nobles cavallers enterrats en els claustres

mentrestant la portera pixa pels escalons
i el marit no pot més i la dona del metge
se'n va i agafa el metge i li diu fill de puta
i se'l fica entre cames i tot es pega foc
i la nena que plora sola a la porteria
i les inscripcions obscenes dels comuns

i el crani rebotant per tots els escalons.

XXII

Like the child with no parents and the parents with no child
and lasses at the pictures, with their legs open wide
and a hand up their skirts, and the rosary told at home,
and there is the navvy killed in a fall from a scaffold
and the man who bakes bread and someone who brings a tape
measure to log the coffin's size appropriately
and like there are tram crews who work throughout the night
on New Year's Eve and sinks with plug holes there is
the lift that waits with its dirty yellowish light
meanwhile the concierge gets wasted on the wine
and pisses down the stairs and her daughter is afraid
and her husband is at it with the doctor's wife
and trams terrify with the clanking of their brakes
and the doctor who devotes his time to cracking nuts
meanwhile the concierge pisses down the stairs
and banging on the doors with a thump from her bust
and the harp player's son, she died three days ago,
who weeps and weeps and lights a candle and sets the candle
in the wine-bottle's top, ogling Sofia Loren
and then the Swiss lass screams out along the corridor
and her cousin behind, candelabra in hand,
and the girl off to bed earlier now than ever
and a chill like a hand makes its way up her thighs
and just for a moment she thinks her bum is cuter
and the neighbours who died poisoned by their food
just the other day and neither wife nor daughter will
touch anything at all as they cry and cry their eyes out
and the Swiss lass and her cousin lie brutally asleep
the candelabra alight and the bedspread alight
and the curtains alight and all the flat alight
the noble knights lie buried in the cloisters

meanwhile the concierge pisses down the stairs
and her husband is worn out and the doctor's wife
goes and grabs the doctor and calls him a fucking bastard
and shoves him between her legs and all goes up in flames
and the wee lass weeps alone outside the porters' lodge
and the etchings obscene on the lavatory walls

and the skull bouncing down every single stair.

Bibliography

Andrés Estellés, Vicent (2014). *L'Hotel París*, in *Obra completa*, I, pp. 223–248. Valencia: Tres i Quatre. (The version used for this translation.)

———. (2014). *El monòleg*, in *Obra completa*, I, pp. 249–260. Valencia: Tres i Quatre.

———. (2014). *Testimoni d'Horaci*, in *Obra completa*, I, pp. 261–289. Valencia: Tres i Quatre.

Backburn, S. (2008). "Being in-itself/for-itself", in *The Oxford Dictionary of Philosophy*. Oxford: Oxford University Press. Retrieved 19 Feb. 2024, from www.oxfordreference.com/view/10.1093/oi/authority.20110803095456283

Bakhtin, M. (1981). "Forms of Time of the Chronotope and in the Novel", in *The Dialogic Imagination*. Austin: University of Texas Press, pp. 84–258.

Baldick, C. (2015). "Chronotope", in *The Oxford Dictionary of Literary Terms*. Oxford: Oxford University Press. Retrieved 21 Feb. 2024, from https://www.oxfordreference.com/view/10.1093/acref/9780198715443.001.0001/acref-9780198715443-e-202.

Buchanan, I. (2018). "Bad faith", in *A Dictionary of Critical Theory*. Oxford: Oxford University Press. Retrieved 20 Feb. 2024, from www.oxfordreference.com/view/10.1093/acref/9780198794790.001.0001/acref-9780198794790-e-62.

Carbó, Ferran (2014). "La poesia de Vicent Andrés Estellés entre el 1952 i el 1958: de les homilies a les tenebres", in Andrés Estellés, *Obra completa*, I. Valencia: Tres i Quatre, pp. 1–63.

Field Levander, C. & Pratt Guterl, M. (2015). *Hotel Life: The Story of a Place Where Anything Can Happen*. Chapel Hill, NC: University of North Carolina Press.

Foucault, Michel (1986). "Of Other Spaces", in *Diacritics*, Vol. 16, No. 1, pp. 22–27.

Fuster, Joan (1962). *Nosaltres, els valencians*, Barcelona: Eds. 62.

Kristeva, J. (1982). *Powers of Horror: An Essay on Abjection*, New York: Colombia University Press.

Moore, Robbie (2021). *Hotel Modernity: Corporate Space in Literature and Film*. Edinburgh: Edinburgh University Press.

Sartre, J. P. (1964). *Huis clos*, London: Methuen.

Thomas, Dylan (2006). *Under Milk Wood*, Project Gutenburg Australia (no page numbers). Retrieved 19 Feb. 2024, from https://gutenberg.net.au/ebooks06/0608221h.html.

Anglophone readers may find the following material in English useful:

Andrés Estellés, Vicent (1992). *Nights That Make the Night: Selected Poems*, translated and edited by David Rosenthal, New York: Persea Books.

———.(2013). *After the Classics*: *Selected Verse*, translated and edited by D. Keown & Tom Owen (IVITRA Research in Linguistics and Literature). Amsterdam: John Benjamins.

Keown, D. (2011). *A Companion to Catalan Studies*. Martlesham: Boydell & Brewer.

———. (2013). "Poems by Vicent Andrés Estellés" in *Translation Review*, vol. 87, pp. 70–88.

———. (2017). "Translate and Assimilate? The Selected Verse of Vicent Andrés Estellés in English." *Journal of Iberian and Latin American Studies*, vol. 23, pp. 85–98.

Mira, Irene (2019). *Teoria crítica de l'espai en la literatura contemporània: aplicació a la lírica de Vicent Andrés Estellés*. Ph D thesis. Universitat d'Alacant. Retrieved Feb. 25, 2024 from https://rua.ua.es/dspace/handle/10045/120146, pp. 265–280.

——— & Salvador V. (2020). "The Scenography of Death in Contemporary Poetry: The Case of Vicent Andrés Estellés", in *Discourses on the Edge of Life*, pp. 167–178. Retrieved 19 Feb. 2024, from https://benjamins.com/catalog/ivitra.26.

Salvador, V. (2022). "The Desired Woman: Portraits of Women in the Poetry of Vicent Andrés Estellés", in *Character and Gender in Contemporary Catalan Literature*, pp. 71–88. Berlin: Peter Lang.

Strubell, M. (2011). "The Catalan Language", in *Companian to Catalan Culture*, ed. by Dominic Keown, pp. 117-142. London: Boydell and Brewer.

CATALAN STUDIES
IN CULTURE AND LINGUISTICS
Edited by Antonio Cortijo Ocaña

Vol. 1   Antonio Cortijo Ocaña / Jordi M. Antolí Martínez (eds.): Approaches to New Trends in Research on Catalan Studies. Linguistics, Literature, Education and Cultural Studies. 2021.

Vol. 2   Marco Antonio Coronel Ramos (ed.): Mito y realidad: investigaciones sobre el pensamiento dual en el mundo occidental. 2022.

Vol. 3   Judit Freixa / M. Isabel Guardiola / Josep Martines / M. Amor Montané (eds.): Dictionarization of Catalan Neologisms. 2022.

Vol. 4   Adolf Piquer / Adéla Koťátková (eds.): Character and Gender in Contemporary Catalan Literature. 2022.

Vol. 5   Alejandro Llinares Planells / Guillermo López Juan (eds.): Rethinking Violence in Valencia and Catalonia. 2024.

Vol. 6   Joan de Déu Martines Llinares: Lèxic i Natura en les narracions d'Enric Valor. 2024.

Vol. 7   Hotel Paris Vicent Andrés Estellés Edition, Foreword and Translation by Dominic Keown. 2024.

www.peterlang.com